IMAGINE
A
JOYFUL
ECONOMY

This book is a welcome addition to the emerging discussions of integrating ecology, economics, politics, ethics, and values. It urges us to rethink how we create thriving social and economic systems for the flourishing of the Earth community. We are indebted to Speth and Denton for articulating these new directions in a clear and accessible manner.

— Mary Evelyn Tucker and John Grim, Directors, Yale Forum on Religion and Ecology and Executive Producers, Journey of the Universe film

JAMES GUSTAVE SPETH
&
PETER DENTON

+ + +

Imagine
a
Joyful
Economy

WOOD LAKE

Editor: Mike Schwartzentruber
Proofreader: Dianne Greenslade
Designer: Robert MacDonald

Library and Archives Canada Cataloguing in Publication
Title: Imagine a joyful economy / James Gustave Speth & Peter Denton.
Names: Speth, James Gustave, author. | Denton, Peter H., 1959- author. |
Container of (work): Speth, James Gustave. Joyful economy. |
Container of (work): Denton, Peter H., 1959- Creation ecology.
Description: Includes bibliographical references.
Identifiers: Canadiana (print) 20190203943 | Canadiana (ebook) 20190203986 |
ISBN 9781773431611 (softcover) | ISBN 9781773431765 (HTML)
Subjects: LCSH: Sustainable development. | LCSH: Sustainable development – Religious
aspects – Christianity. | LCSH: Economic development – Environmental aspects. |
LCSH: Environmental responsibility. | LCSH: Environmental responsibility – Economic
aspects. | LCSH: Environmental responsibility – Religious aspects – Christianity. |
LCSH: Environmental protection. | LCSH: Environmental protection – Economic aspects. |
LCSH: Environmental protection – Religious aspects – Christianity.
Classification: LCC HC79.E5 I43 2020 | DDC 338.9/27–dc23

ISBN 978-1-77343-161-1

Published by Wood Lake Publishing Inc.
485 Beaver Lake Road, Kelowna, BC, Canada, V4V 1S5
www.woodlake.com | 250.766.2778

Wood Lake Publishing acknowledges the financial support of
the Government of Canada. Wood Lake Publishing acknowledges the financial support of
the Province of British Columbia through the Book Publishing Tax Credit.

Wood Lake Publishing acknowledges that we operate in the unceded territory of
the Syilx/Okanagan People, and we work to support reconciliation and challenge the
legacies of colonialism. The Syilx/Okanagan territory is a diverse and beautiful
landscape of deserts and lakes, alpine forests and endangered grasslands.
We honour the ancestral stewardship of the Syilx/Okanagan People.

Printed in Canada
Printing 10 9 8 7 6 5 4 3 2 1

TABLE OF CONTENTS

JAMES GUSTAVE SPETH

+ + +

The Joyful Economy

A
NEXT
SYSTEM
POSSIBILITY

+ + +

Introduction

In his 1976 book *The Joyless Economy*, Tibor Scitovsky saw environmental neglect and other problems as results of a very American pattern of "putting the earning of money ahead of the enjoyment of life."[1] More than four decades later, his observation remains valid.

In this essay, I will explore the transition from a joyless economy to a *joyful* one. In the joyful economy, the goal of economic life is to sustain, nourish, and restore human and natural communities so that the material and non-material blessings of life are available to all. It is a new system of political economy that gives true and honest priority not to profit, production, and power, but rather to people, place, and planet. Its watchword is caring – caring for each other, for the natural world, and for the future. I will argue that promoting the transition to such a new political economy should be the central task of a new environmentalism.

To guide us, we desperately need a new American Dream – a dream of an America where the pursuit of happiness is sought not in more getting and spending, but in the growth of human solidarity, devoted friendship, and meaningful accomplishment; where the average person is empowered to achieve his or her human potential; where the benefits of economic activity are widely and equitably shared; where democracy and civic participation flourish at all levels; where the environment is sustained for current and future generations; and, where the virtues of simple living, community self-reliance, good fellowship, and respect for nature predominate. These traditions do not always prevail today, but they are not dead. They await us, and indeed they are currently being awakened across America.

"More than a little utopian," some may be thinking. Yes, but a utopian vision is precisely what today's situation requires. Things are much too bad for pessimism, it has been noted. And as Richard Flanagan asked recently, "What reality was ever created by realists?...What we cannot dream we can never do."[2]

The environmentalist's tale

There are many areas of public concern that can frame the case for this economic and political transformation to a new system of political economy.[3] I will present the environmental one.

A half-century has flown by since a group of us launched the Natural Resources Defense Council (NRDC). Over that period, NRDC and other mainstream U.S. environmental groups have racked up more victories and accomplishments than one can count. I shudder to think what our world would be like had they not.

Yet, despite those accomplishments, a spectre is haunting American environmentalism – the spectre of failure. All of us who have been part of the environmental movement in the United States must now face up to a deeply troubling paradox: our environmental organizations have grown in strength and sophistication, but the environment has continued to go downhill. The prospect of a ruined planet is now very real. We have won many victories, but we are losing the planet.

Climate change is coming at us very hard. A great tragedy is now likely. Around the world, we are losing biodiversity, forests, fisheries, and agricultural soils at frightening rates. Fresh water shortages multiply. Toxics accumulate in ecosystems, and in us.[4]

But those are global-scale issues, some say; we have done better here at home. In some ways that is true, but the reality is that our domestic environmental challenges are far from met. Half of the fresh water bodies in the U.S. still do not meet the goal of "fishable and swimmable" set for 1983 in the 1972 Clean Water Act.[5] And about half of Americans suffer from unhealthy levels of air pollutants.[6]

We have protected an area the size of California as designated wilderness, but since 1982 we have lost open space fully the size of Washington state to development – urban and industrial sprawl – much of it prime agricultural land.[7] Thirty percent of U.S. plants and 18 percent of our animals are now threatened with extinction.[8] And these estimates do not take into account the full impacts of likely climate change. America's record of climate inaction must rank as the greatest dereliction of civic responsibility in the history of the Republic.

Something is terribly wrong. Clearly more of the same cannot be the answer. We've had decades of more of the same.

Here we are, five decades after the burst of energy and hope at the first Earth Day, headed toward the very planetary conditions we set out to prevent. Indeed, all we have to do – to destroy the planet's climate, impoverish its biota, and poison its people – is to keep doing exactly what we are doing today, with no growth in the human population or the world economy. Just continue to release greenhouse gases at current rates, just continue to degrade ecosystems and release toxic chemicals at current rates, and the world in the latter part of this century won't be fit to live in. But human activities are not holding at current levels – they are accelerating, dramatically. It took all of human history to grow the $7 trillion world economy of 1950. Now, we grow by that amount in a decade. The potential for much larger and continuing environmental losses is very real.

American environmentalists must take some responsibility for what has happened. In particular, we did not take stock and adjust to the dangerous new conditions ushered in by the

Reagan revolution of 1980. As I will discuss, that was a moment to reassess and reboot.

But our part of the blame is decidedly the lesser part. To chronicle the much larger part, it is useful to begin with Frederick Buell and his valuable book *From Apocalypse to Way of Life*. He writes the following:

> Something happened to strip the environmental [cause] of what seemed in the 1970s to be its self-evident inevitability ... In reaction to the decade of crisis, a strong and enormously successful anti-environmental disinformation industry sprang up. It was so successful that it helped midwife a new phase in the history of US environmental politics, one in which an abundance of environmental concern was nearly blocked by an equal abundance of anti-environmental contestation.[9]

Nowhere has this disinformation campaign been more important – and successful – than with climate change, all brilliantly documented in Naomi Oreskes and Erik Conway's book *Merchants of Doubt*.[10]

The disinformation industry that Buell notes was part of a larger picture of opposition. That reaction can perhaps be dated from Lewis Powell's famous 1971 memorandum to the U.S. Chamber of Commerce, in which he urges business to fight back against environmental and other regulations. Powell, then a corporate attorney who would become a Supreme Court justice, urged corporations to get more involved in policy and politics. Since then, well-funded forces of resistance and opposition have arisen. Especially since Reagan became president, virtually every step forward has been hard fought. It is not just environmental protection that has been forcefully attacked, but essentially all progressive causes, even the basic idea of government action in the interests of the people as a whole.

The story of the conservative assault on environmental protections has now been well told in Judith Layzer's important 2012 book, *Open for Business*.

> Since the 1970s, conservative activists have disseminated a compelling anti-regulatory storyline to counter the environmentalist narrative, mobilized grassroots opposition to environmental regulations, and undertaken sophisticated legal challenges to the basis for and implementation of environmental laws. Over time, these activities have imparted legitimacy to a new anti-regulatory rhetoric, one that emphasizes distrust of the federal bureaucracy, admiration for unfettered private property rights and markets, skepticism about science, and disdain for environmental advocates. By employing arguments rooted in this formula, conservatives have been instrumental in blocking efforts to pass major new environmental legislation or increase the stringency of existing laws.[11]

A constantly building opposition is, to my way of thinking, the obvious, immediate reason for our mounting environmental failure. But this exercise of power and control is, as I will discuss, merely the surface political manifestation of deeper systemic imperatives.

Here is the biggest mistake I believe we environmentalists made. As federal environmental laws and programs burst onto the scene in the early 1970s, we eagerly pursued the important goals and avenues those laws opened up. There, the path to success was clear. But in doing so we left by the wayside the more difficult and deeper challenges highlighted by leading environmental thinkers of the 1960s and 1970s – Barry Commoner, Paul Ehrlich, Donella Meadows, and others.[12] Their overall point was that we should strike at the root causes of environmental decline. They saw that doing so would require us to seek fundamental changes in our prevailing system of political economy – to proceed down the path of system change. They saw that the problem was the system.

Most of us ignored these calls for systemic change. In particular, we should have revisited these deeper issues when our momentum stalled after 1980, especially in light of the anti-environmentalism of the Reagan years. What happened instead was that the successes of the 1970s locked us into patterns of environmental action that have since proved no match for the system we're up against. New laws created major opportunities to make large environmental gains. But in pursuing these changes, we were drawn ever more completely inside the D.C. Beltway. Once there, inside the system, we were compelled to a certain tameness by the need to succeed. As Washington became more conservative, mainstream environmentalists became more cautious. In sum, we opted to work within the system of political economy that we found, and we neglected to seek transformation of the system itself.

The central precept has been that the current system can be made to work for the environment. America has run a half-century experiment testing whether this is true. The results are now in, and we have learned that our system of political economy does not work well, to put it mildly, when it comes to the environment.

Today's environmentalism is fine as far as it goes. The problem has been the absence of huge, complementary investments of time, energy, and money in other, deeper approaches to change. And here, the leading environmental organizations must be faulted for not doing nearly enough to ensure these investments in system change were made.

System change is essential because our environmental problems are actually rooted in the defining features of our current political economy. These include the following:

■ *an unquestioning society-wide commitment to economic growth at virtually any cost;*

- *a measure of growth – GDP – that includes not only the good but also the bad and the ugly;*

- *powerful corporate interests whose overriding objective is to generate profit and grow, including profit from avoiding the social and environmental costs they create;*

- *markets that systematically fail to recognize these costs unless corrected by government; government that is subservient to corporate interests and the growth imperative;*

- *rampant consumerism spurred endlessly by sophisticated advertising;*

- *social injustice and economic insecurity so vast that they paralyze action and empower often false claims that needed measures would cost jobs and hurt the economy; and,*

- *economic activity now so large in scale that its impacts alter the fundamental biophysical operations of the planet.*

All these combine to deliver an ever-growing economy that is undermining the ability of the planet to sustain human and natural communities.

It is clearly time for something different – a new environmentalism. And here is the core of this new environmentalism: it seeks a new economy. To deliver on the promise of a new system, we must build a new politics. New environmental leaders will learn from the ideas of the 1960s and early 1970s, rediscover environmentalism's original roots, and step outside the system in order to change it before it is too late.

We must ask again the basic question, "What is an environmental issue?" Air and water pollution, of course. But what if the right answer is that environmental issues include anything that determines environmental outcomes? Then, surely, the creeping plutocracy and corporatocracy we face – the ascendancy of money power and corporate power over people power – these are environmental issues. And more: the chartering and empowering of artificial persons to do virtually anything in the name of profit and growth – that is the very nature of today's corporation; the fetish of GDP growth as the ultimate public good and the main aim of government; our runaway consumerism; our vast social insecurity with half of U.S. families living paycheque to paycheque. These are among the underlying drivers of environmental outcomes. They are environmental concerns, imperative ones, but they rarely appear on the agendas of our main national environmental groups.

The agenda of the new environmentalism should embrace a profound challenge to consumerism and commercialism and the lifestyles they offer; a turning away from "growthmania" and a profit-centred economy; a redefinition of what society should be striving to grow; a challenge to corporate dominance and a redefinition of the corporation and its goals; a commitment to deep change in both the reach of the market and the ownership of productive assets; and, a powerful assault on the materialistic, anthropocentric, and contempocentric values that currently dominate American culture.

Environmentalists must also join with social progressives in addressing the crisis of inequality and deprivation now unravelling America's social fabric. Similarly, environmentalists must make common cause with those seeking to reform politics and strengthen democracy. What we have seen in the United States is the emergence of a vicious circle: income disparities shift political access and influence to wealthy constituencies and large businesses, which further imperils the potential of the democratic process to act to correct the growing income disparities. Environmentalists need to embrace public financing of elections; new anticorruption ethical restrictions on legislatures; the right to vote; tougher regulation of lobbying and of revolving door, nonpartisan congressional redistricting; and other political reform measures as core to their agenda. We must join in campaigns like Move to Amend, to forge a new Constitution that recognizes that corporations are not people and money is not speech.

The new environmentalism must work with a progressive coalition to build a mighty force in electoral politics. This will require major efforts of grassroots organizing, strengthening groups working at the state and community levels, and supporting and fielding candidates for public office. It will also require developing motivational messages and appeals. Our environmental discourse has thus far been dominated by lawyers, scientists, and economists. Now, we need to hear a lot more from the poets, preachers, philosophers, and psychologists.

Above all, the new environmental politics must be broadly inclusive, reaching out to embrace the concerns of working families and union members, people of colour, frontline communities, religious organizations, the women's movement, and other communities of complementary interest and shared fate. Much stronger alliances are needed, alliances powerful enough to overcome the "silo effect" that separates the environmental community from those working on domestic political reforms, a progressive social agenda, gender equality, racial justice, international peace, consumer issues, world health and population concerns, and world poverty and underdevelopment.

The final goal of the new environmental politics must be to "build the movement." Environmentalists are still said to be part of "the environmental movement." We need a real one – networked together with other progressives – protesting, demanding action and accountability from governments and corporations, and taking steps as consumers and communities to realize sustainability and social justice in everyday life. Today we see the strengthening of many movements but not yet the fusion of movements across issues. We need the long-awaited movement of movements.

System change

In my books I have endeavoured to make the case for driving systemic changes so deeply that our country emerges with a new system of political economy, one programmed to routinely deliver good results for people, place, and planet. I know that the idea of a new political economy is too big to swallow whole. System change can best be approached, I think, through a series of interacting, mutually reinforcing transitions – transformations that attack and undermine the key motivational structures of the current system, while replacing these old structures with new arrangements needed for a flourishing of human and natural communities.

I believe the following transitions hold the key to moving to a new and joyful political economy. We can think of each as a progression from today to tomorrow. In each of these areas, there are currently laws and policies that shape today's realities. Collectively, we can think of these laws as the law of today's corporatist, consumerist capitalism. What we should be moving toward is the law of the next system, beyond today's capitalism and yesterday's socialism.

■ THE MARKET: *We should be moving from near laissez-faire to powerful market governance in the public interest; from dishonest prices to honest ones and from unfair wages to fair ones;*

from commodification to reclaiming the commons, the things that rightfully belong to all of us.

■ THE CORPORATION: *We should be moving from shareholder primacy to stakeholder primacy, from one dominant ownership and profit-driven model to new business models embracing economic democracy and goals other than profit; and from private to public control of major investment decisions.*

■ ECONOMIC GROWTH: *We should be moving from growth fetish to post-growth society, from mere GDP-growth to growth in social and environmental well-being, and growth focused squarely on democratically determined priorities.*

■ MONEY AND FINANCE: *We should be moving from Wall Street to Main Street, from money created through bank debt to money created by government; from investments seeking high financial returns to those seeking high social and environmental returns.*

■ SOCIAL CONDITIONS: *We should be moving from economic insecurity to security; from vast inequalities to fundamental fairness; from racial, religious, and other invidious discrimination to just and tolerant treatment of all groups.*

■ INDICATORS: *We should be moving from GDP ("grossly distorted picture") to accurate measures of social and environmental health and quality of life.*

■ CONSUMERISM: *We should be moving from consumerism and affluenza to sufficiency and mindful consumption, from more to enough.*

■ COMMUNITIES: *We should be moving from runaway enterprise and throwaway communities to vital local economies, from social rootlessness to rootedness and human solidarity.*

■ DOMINANT CULTURAL VALUES: *We should be moving from having to being, from getting to giving, from richer to better, from isolated to connected, from apart-from-nature to part-of-nature, from near-term to long-term.*

■ POLITICS: *We should be moving from weak democracy to strong, from creeping corporatocracy and plutocracy to true popular sovereignty and empowerment of marginalized groups.*

■ FOREIGN POLICY AND THE MILITARY: *We should be moving from American exceptionalism to America as a normal nation, from hard power to soft, from military prowess to real security.*

The good news is that we already know a great deal about the policy and other changes needed to move strongly in these directions.[13] Even better, we are already seeing the proliferation of innovative models along many of the lines sketched here, particularly at the local level: sustainable communities, transition towns, solidarity and local living economies, sustainable and regenerative agriculture, new regional and organic food systems, locally owned and managed renewable energy, and community development and investment institutions. We are also seeing the spread of innovative business models that prioritize community and environment over profit and growth – including social enterprises, for-benefit business, worker-owned and other cooperatives, and local credit unions – as well as numerous campaigns for fair wages, worker rights, and pro-family policies.[14] Together with new community-oriented and earth-friendly lifestyles, these initiatives provide inspirational models of how things might work in a new political economy devoted to sustaining human and natural communities. Practical utopians at work and play, bringing the future into the present!

A change in values

In describing these transitions, I have stressed the centrality of new values and the evolution to a new consciousness. I would never say that no progress can be made until America's dominant culture has been transformed. But I do believe that we won't get far in addressing our major challenges unless there is a parallel, ongoing transformation in values and culture.

To elaborate, our dominant culture should shift, from today to tomorrow, in the following ways:

   ▪ *Instead of viewing humanity as something apart from nature, and nature as something to be transcended and dominated, we will see ourselves as part of nature, as offspring of its evolutionary process, as close kin to wild things, and as wholly dependent on its vitality and the services it provides.*

■ Rather than seeing nature as humanity's resource to exploit as it sees fit for economic and other purposes, we will see the natural world as holding intrinsic value independent of people and as having rights that create the duty of ecological stewardship.

■ We will no longer discount the future by focusing so intently on the short term, but instead take the long view and recognize our duties to human and natural communities well into the future. Instead of today's hyperindividualism and social isolation, we will reward those who foster a powerful sense of community, conviviality, and social solidarity, in all venues from local to cosmopolitan.

■ Violence will no longer be glorified nor wars easily accepted. The spreading of hate and invidious divisions will be frowned on and will no longer be a launching pad for careers in broadcasting and politics. Women's and LGBTTQ+ rights and racial and ethnic justice will be realized in everyday life.

■ Materialism, consumerism, and the primacy of ever more possessions will give way to a culture that grants priority to family and personal relationships, learning, experiencing nature, service, spirituality, and living within Earth's limits.

■ Rather than tolerate gross economic, social, gender, racial, and political inequality, we will demand and achieve a high measure of equality in all of these spheres.

Here's an often-overlooked fact – we don't need to wait on these changes but can bring them about. "The central conservative truth is that culture, not politics, determines the success of a society," Daniel Patrick Moynihan remarked. "The central liberal truth is that politics can change a culture and save it from itself."[15]

We actually know important things about how values and culture can change. One sure path to cultural change is, unfortunately, the cataclysmic event – the crisis – that profoundly challenges prevailing values and can delegitimize the status quo. The Great Depression is the classic example. I think we can be confident that we haven't seen the end of major crises, but they will drive events in the right directions only if we are prepared.

Two other key factors in cultural change are leadership and social narrative, as Howard Gardner has observed.

Whether they are heads of a nation or senior officials of the United Nations, leaders ... have enormous potential to change minds ... and in the process they can change the course of history ...

I have suggested one way to capture the attention of a disparate population: by creating a compelling story, embodying that story in one's own life, and presenting the story in many different formats so that it can eventually topple the counter-stories in one's culture. The story must be simple, easy to identify with, emotionally resonant, and evocative of positive experiences.[16]

Bill Moyers, a powerful force for good in our country, has also written about this.

> America needs a different story ... the leaders and thinkers and activists who honestly tell that story and speak passionately of the moral and religious values it puts in play will be the first political generation since the New Deal to win power back for the people.[17]

There is some evidence that Americans are ready for another story. Large majorities of Americans, when polled, express disenchantment with today's lifestyles and offer support for values similar to those urged here.[18] (Of course, respondents do not always act on the high-minded sentiments expressed to pollsters.)

Another key source of value change is social movements. Social movements are all about consciousness raising, and if successful, they can help usher in a new consciousness.

Another way forward to a new consciousness lies with the world's religions. Mary Evelyn Tucker has noted that "no other group of institutions can wield the particular moral authority of the religions."[19] The potential of faith communities is enormous, and they are turning more attention to issues of social justice, peace, and environment. Spiritual awakening to new values and new consciousness can also derive from the arts, literature, philosophy, and science.

Consider, for example, the long tradition of "reverence for life" stretching back to the Emperor Ashoka more than 2,200 years ago and forward to Albert Schweitzer, Aldo Leopold, Thomas Berry, E. O. Wilson, Terry Tempest Williams, and others.[20]

Education, of course, can also contribute enormously to cultural change. Here one should include education in the largest sense, embracing not only formal education but also day-to-day and experiential education, as well as the fast-developing field of social marketing. Social marketing has had notable successes in moving people away from bad behaviours such as smoking and drunk driving, and its approaches could be applied to these themes as well.

A major and very hopeful path is seeding the landscape with innovative, instructive models. As noted, there is a proliferation of innovative models of community revitalization and business enterprise. Local currencies, slow money, state Genuine Progress Indicators, locavores – these are bringing the future into the present in very concrete ways. These actual models will grow in importance as communities search for answers on how the future should look, and they can change minds. Seeing is believing.

In sum, cultural transformation won't be easy; but it's not impossible, either.

Joy

The fundamental importance of these changes in values and culture is underscored by the findings of the relatively new field of positive psychology. Studies that compare levels of happiness and life satisfaction among nations at different stages of economic income find that the citizens of wealthier countries do report higher levels of life satisfaction. Yet the correlation between income and life satisfaction is rather poor, and it is even poorer when factors such as quality of government are statistically controlled. And this positive relationship virtually disappears when one looks only at countries with GDP per capita over $10,000 per year. In short, once a country achieves a moderate level of income, further growth does not significantly improve perceived well-being.[21]

Even more challenging to the idea that well-being increases with higher incomes are extensive time-series data showing that throughout almost the entire post-World War II period, as incomes skyrocketed in the United States and other advanced economies, reported life satisfaction and happiness levels stagnated or even declined slightly. The consistency of this finding across a broad range of societies is impressive.[22] After reviewing the new evidence, Richard Easterlin and Laura Angelescu conclude that "there is no significant relationship between the improvement in happiness and the long-term rate of growth of GDP per capita."[23]

But that is not all. Ed Diener and Martin Seligman, two leaders in positive psychology, note the following.

Even more disparity [between income and well-being] shows up when ill-being measures are considered. For instance, depression rates have increased 10-fold over the same 50-year period, and rates of anxiety are also rising ... There is [also] a decreasing level of social connectedness in society, as evidenced by declining levels of trust in other people and in governmental institutions.[24]

You may have heard the joke: "Those who say money can't buy happiness just don't know where to shop!" But the truth is that the data indicate that money can't buy joy or satisfaction in life among the more affluent. Study after study show that there is a sharply declining marginal utility to extra income. Diener and Seligman put it this way:

Economic growth seems to have topped out in its capacity to produce more well-being in developed nations ... Efforts and policies to raise income in wealthy nations are unlikely to increase well-being and might even undermine factors (such as rewarding social relationships or other cherished values) that have higher leverage for producing enhanced well-being.[25]

If incomes are such weak generators of well-being in our more affluent societies, what are the things that really do produce happiness and well-being? The answer is somewhat complicated, but when a founder of the field of positive psychology was asked to state briefly the lessons of positive psychology, his answer was, "Other people."[26] We flourish in a setting of warm, nurturing, and rewarding interpersonal relationships, and within that context we flourish best when we are giving, not getting.

The joyful economy

Envisioning a better alternative is the first step in realizing it. Can we begin to envision the contours and texture of daily life in the joyful economy? We can certainly draw on what numerous communities are striving to do today, and there is an extensive literature on transition towns, intentional communities, new enterprise forms, and more.[27] Pointers can also be drawn from the findings of positive psychology and our understanding of national and local needs in many areas. When all this is pulled together, we can see that life in the joyful economy will tend strongly in the following directions.

LOCAL LIFE

Economic and social life will be rooted in the community and the region. More production will be local and regional, with shorter, less-complex supply chains, especially but not only in food and energy supply. Enterprises will be more committed to the long-term well-being of employees and the viability of their communities and will be supported by local, complementary currencies and local financial institutions. People will live closer to work and walk and bike more. Energy production will be decentralized, typically with local ownership and management, and overwhelmingly renewable. Socially, community bonds will be strong; neighbours and genuine, unpretentious relationships important; civic associations and community service groups plentiful; support for teachers and caregivers high. Personal security, tolerance of difference, and empathy will be impressive. Local governance will stress participatory, direct, and deliberative democracy. Citizens will be seized with the responsibility to manage and extend the commons – the valuable assets that belong to everyone – through community land trusts and otherwise.

NEW BUSINESS MODELS

Locally owned businesses, including worker-, customer-, and community-owned firms will be prominent. So too will hybrid business models such as profit/nonprofit and public/private hybrids. Many will be cooperatives, large and small. Everywhere, the profit motive will become secondary, often fading entirely, and social and public missions of many varieties will guide enterprises. Investments, frequently promoting import-substitution, will be locally sourced. Business incubators will help entrepreneurs with arranging finance, technical assistance, and other support. Enterprises of all types will stress environmental and social responsibility.

PLENITUDE

Consumerism will be supplanted by the search for abundance in things that truly bring happiness and joy – family, friends, the natural world, meaningful work. Recognition will go to those who earn trust and provide needed services to the community. Individuals and communities will enjoy a strong rebirth of re-skilling, crafting, and self-provisioning. Overconsumption will be considered vulgar and will be replaced by new investment in civic culture, natural amenities, ecological restoration, education, and community development.

MORE EQUALITY

Because large inequalities are at the root of so many social and environmental problems, measures will be implemented to ensure much greater equality not only of opportunity but also of outcomes. Because life will be simpler, more caring and less grasping, and people less status-conscious, a fairer sharing of economic resources will come naturally. Livelihoods will be secure, including through measures such as a guaranteed living income for all.

REAL DEMOCRACY

Popular sovereignty and government of, by, and for the people will prevail at all levels. Participatory, direct, and deliberative democracy will be commonplace. Following the principle of subsidiarity, government actions will be taken at the smallest, least centralized level that can be effective. Local and regional authorities will be vital in political life, and the saying "the nation-state is too big for the little things and too little for the big things" will be followed in practice.

TIME REGAINED

Formal work hours will be cut back, freeing up time for family, friends, hobbies, household productions, continuing education, skills development, caregiving, volunteering, sports, outdoor recreation, and participating in the arts. Life will be less frenetic. Frugality and thrift will be prized and wastefulness shunned. Mindfulness and living simply with less clutter will carry the day. As a result, social bonds will strengthen. The overlapping webs of encounter and participation that were once hallmarks of America, a nation of joiners, will have been rebuilt. Trust in each other will be high.

NEW GOODS AND SERVICES

Products will be more durable, versatile, and easy to repair, with components that can be reused or recycled. Applying the principles of industrial ecology, the negative impacts of products throughout their life cycles will be minimized, and production systems will be designed to mimic biological ones, with waste eliminated or becoming a useful input elsewhere. The provision of services will replace the purchase of many goods; and sharing, collaborative consumption, and community ownership will be commonplace. Fewer people will buy, and more will prefer to lend and lease and to make and grow their own.

RESONANCE WITH NATURE

Energy will be used with maximum efficiency. Zero discharge of traditional pollutants, toxins, and greenhouse gases will be the norm. Green chemistry will replace the use of toxins and hazardous substances. Organic farming will eliminate pesticide and herbicide use. Prices will reflect the true environmental and social costs of the products we consume. Schools will stress environmental education and pursue "no child left inside" programs. Natural areas and zones of high ecological significance will be protected. Environmental restoration and cleanup programs will be focuses of community concern. There will be a palpable sense that all economic and social activity is nested in the natural world. Biophilic design will bring nature into our buildings and our communities.[28]

GROWTH OFF, CHILDREN ON THE PEDESTAL

Growth in GDP and its local and regional variants will not be seen as a priority; GDP will be seen as a misleading measure of well-being and progress. Instead, indicators of community wealth creation – including measures of social and natural capital – will be closely watched. Special attention will be given to children and young people. Their education and receipt of loving care, shelter, good nutrition and health care, and an environment free of toxins and violence will be our measures of how well we're doing in our communities and as a nation.

SCALE AND RESILIENCE

Society and economy and the enterprises within them will not be too big to understand, appreciate, or manage successfully. Key motivations will be to maintain a human scale and resilience – the capacity to absorb disturbance and outside shocks without disastrous consequences.

GLOBALISM

Despite the many ways life will be more local, and in defiance of the resulting temptation to parochialism, people will feel a

sense of citizenship at larger levels of social and political organization, including, importantly, a powerful sense of global
citizenship. In particular, there will be a deep appreciation of
the need to bring political accountability and democratic control to the many things that can be done only at national and
international levels.

It is important to remember that there are many visions of
successful new economies and next systems. The one I have
sketched here comes closest to what Paul Raskin has described
as "Arcadia." But the joyful economy also includes features of
what Raskin calls "Agoria," which builds on the best features
of modern social democracy, and "Ecodemia," which takes economic democracy as its premise and stresses worker ownership and socialized control of investment decisions.[29]

Having sketched possible life in the next system, it is nev-
ertheless true that we know a lot more about the desired
directionality of change than we do about the ultimate destination. Some may be most comfortable with settling for just that.
It is useful, then, to sketch the questions we can ask to decide
whether we are at least headed in the right directions. Following are 24 questions I think are important in this context.[30]

Questions that can help point us toward a new system

ECONOMY

1. Does the initiative move an ever-larger share of the economy away from the profit motive?

2. Does the initiative assert ever more democratic control over financial investment decisions and the creation of money?

3. Does the initiative diversify the ownership of productive assets and businesses through public enterprises, public-private hybrids, cooperative enterprises, and other forms of economic democracy?

4. Does the initiative increase wealth among the many, rather than accumulating it among the few?

5. Does the initiative promote a new world of locally- and employee-controlled, earth-friendly, and cooperative enterprises rather than further entrench large corporations?

6. Does the initiative assert more democratic control over the actions, size, governance, and motivations of large corporations?

7. Does the initiative promote the growth and health of the commons rather than commodification, commercialism, and capture of commons assets by for-profit corporations?

8. Does the initiative promote limiting the market to what it does well?

9. Does the initiative move away from the growth fetish, GDP worship, and efforts at aggregate economic stimulus, and toward policies that invest in and otherwise promote discrete, democratically determined priorities, high social and environmental returns, and alternative indicators of human and environmental wellbeing and progress at various levels?

POLITY

10. Does the initiative increase decentralization and the diffusion of power, both economic and political, rather than their concentration? Does it respect the principle of subsidiarity? Does it favour democratic governance at the local and regional levels?

11. Does the initiative reverse the evident trends toward corporatocracy and plutocracy, reassert people power over money power, and reclaim government by, for, and of the people – real democracy at all levels, from local to global?

12. Does the initiative enhance human freedom and protect both liberty and privacy?

13. Does the initiative recognize the important role of planning in successful governmental undertakings?

14. Does the initiative contribute to the ongoing strengthening of the movement for deep change?

15. Does the initiative contribute to a more just, peaceful situation internationally rather than the opposite?

SOCIETY

16. Does the initiative increase not only equality of opportunity but also actual social and economic equality, including the elimination of poverty?

17. Does the initiative promote community, solidarity, care, and inclusion rather than strife, division, and social neglect?

18. Does the initiative strengthen children and families, rather than weaken them?

19. Does the initiative celebrate diversity of all forms rather than promote marginalization, discrimination, or homogenization?

20. Does the initiative work against consumerism, materialism, and "affluenza" rather than depend on them? Does the initiative embrace the maxim "work and spend less, create and connect more"?

ENVIRONMENT

21. Does the initiative envision the economy as nested in and dependent on the world of nature, its resources, and its systems of life?

22. Does the initiative recognize the rights of species other than humans and otherwise transcend anthropocentrism?

23. Does the initiative recognize that environmental success depends on correcting the underlying drivers of environmental decline and working for deep, systemic change outside the current framework of environmental law and policy?

24. Does the initiative respond to global-scale environmental challenges through innovative approaches like the establishment of a World Environment Organization that is every bit as powerful as the World Trade Organization?

To conclude this discussion, one cannot do better than to quote from the remarkable John Maynard Keynes. He was also thinking about possible futures in his 1933 essay "Economic Possibilities for Our Grandchildren." There, he envisioned the day much like ours today, when the economy could provide a decent standard of living for all. Then, he wrote this:

For the first time since his creation man will be faced with his real, his permanent problem – how to use his freedom from pressing economic cares, how to occupy [his] leisure ... how to live wisely and agreeably and well…When the accumulation of wealth is no longer of high social importance, there will be great changes in the code of morals. The love of money as a possession ... will be recognized for what it is, a somewhat disgusting morbidity, one of those semi-criminal, semi-pathological propensities which one hands over with a shudder to the specialists ...

I see us free, therefore, to return to some of the most sure and certain principles of religion and traditional virtue – that avarice is a vice, that the exaction of usury is a misdemeanour, and the love of money is detestable, that those who walk most truly in the paths of virtue and sane wisdom take least thought for the morrow. We shall once more value ends above means and prefer the good to the useful. We shall honour those who can teach us how to pluck the hour and the day virtuously and well, the delightful people who are capable of taking direct enjoyment in things ... Chiefly, do not let us overestimate the importance of the economic problem, or sacrifice to its supposed necessities other matters of greater and more permanent significance.[31]

How might it happen?

In thinking about the need for transformation, I have had to think about a "theory of change" – how transformative change can happen. The theory embraces the seminal role of crises in waking us from the slumber of routine and in shining the spotlight on the failings of the current order of things. It puts great stock in transformative leadership that can point beyond the crisis to something better. The theory adopts the view that systemic changes must be driven both bottom-up and top-down – from communities, businesses, and citizens deciding on their own to build the future locally as well as to develop the political muscle to adopt system-changing policies at the national and international levels. And it sees a powerful citizens' movement as a necessary spur to action at all levels.

Here is how it might all come together. As conditions

continue to decline across a wide front, or at best fester as they are, ever-larger numbers of people lose faith in the current system and its ability to deliver on the values it proclaims. The system steadily loses support, leading to a crisis of legitimacy. Meanwhile, traditional crises, both in the economy and in the environment, grow more numerous and fearsome. In response, progressives of all stripes coalesce, find their voice and their strength, and pioneer the development of a powerful set of new ideas and policy proposals confirming that the path to a better world does indeed exist. Demonstrations and protests multiply, and a powerful movement for pro-democracy reform and transformative change is born. At the local level, people and groups come together to take control of their communities' futures and thus plant the seeds of change through a host of innovative initiatives that provide inspirational models of how things might work in a new political economy devoted to sustaining human and natural communities. Sensing the direction in which the current is moving, our wiser and more responsible leaders, political and otherwise, rise to the occasion, support the growing movement for change, and frame a compelling story or narrative that makes sense of it all and provides a positive vision of a better future for all. It is a moment of democratic possibility.

One sure sign that the search for a new political economy has begun is the way that constituencies have formed around new concepts of the economy – including the solidarity economy, the caring economy, the sharing economy, the restorative economy, the regenerative economy, the sustaining economy, the commons economy, the resilient economy, and, of course, the new economy. There is ongoing discussion of the need for a "next system" and a "great transition" and for a "just transition" rooted in racial, gender, and class justice. In 2012, the most searched words on the Merriam-Webster site were "capitalism" and "socialism."

Under whatever names, the needed transformations require institutions to promote them. Existing institutions like the Democracy Collaborative, the Institute for Policy Studies, the Tellus Institute, *Yes!* magazine, the Capital Institute, Friends of the Earth, People's Action, the Labor Network for Sustainability, Jobs with Justice, the National Domestic Workers Alliance, Chelsea Green Publishing, the Institute for Local Self-Reliance, among others, have taken up the cause, as have organizations strengthening new types of businesses such as the Business Alliance for Local Living Economies and the American Sustainable Business Council. Joining them are a series of new entities seeking to bring the many "new economy" issues and organizations together, including the New Economy Coalition (at this time, more than 200 organizations have already joined the New Economy Coalition) and the Next System Project that I co-chair. Finally, there are a number of impressive new economy groups with a focus on the law. Here, I would mention the Sustainable Economies

Law Center, the Community Environmental Legal Defense Fund, the Earth Law Center, and the New Economy Law Center at the Vermont Law School. This is important work, and it is a privilege to be involved in it.

Whether driven by climate and fossil fuel insults; poverty, low wages, and joblessness; deportation of immigrants and other family issues; treatment of women; or voter suppression, movements are now challenging key aspects of the system, seeking to drive deep change beyond incremental reform, and offering alternative visions and new paths forward. There are groups that are marching in the streets, state capitals, and local congressional offices. Others are starting to run people for office around alternative agendas. There are places where the needed research is occurring, and new coalitions are bringing diverse groups together. Strong movements can be found in other countries, and, indeed, many countries are further along than we Americans are. These are among the grounds for hope, the reasons to believe that real change is possible.

I hope today's young people will not worry unduly about being thought "radical" and will find ways to short-circuit the long and tortuous path I took. If it seems right to you, embrace it. A wonderful group of leaders and activists who are trying to change the system for the better are building new communities in which we all can participate.

APPENDIX

+ + +

New Systems

Possibilities and Proposals

Truly addressing the problems of the 21st century requires going beyond business as usual – it requires "changing the system." But what does this mean? And what would it entail?

The inability of traditional politics and policies to address fundamental U.S. challenges has generated an increasing number of thoughtful proposals that suggest new possibilities. Individual thinkers have begun to set out – sometimes in considerable detail – alternatives that emphasize fundamental change in our system of politics and economics.

We at the Next System Project – www.nextsystem.org – want to help dispel the wrongheaded idea that "there is no alternative." To that end, we have been gathering some of the most interesting and important proposals for political-economic alternatives – in effect, descriptions of new systems. Some are more detailed than others, but each seeks to envision something very different from today's political economy.

We have been working with their authors on the basis of a comparative framework – available on our website – aimed at encouraging them to elaborate their visions to include not only core economic institutions but also, as far as is possible, political structure, cultural dimensions, transition pathways, and so forth.

Individually and collectively, these papers challenge the deadly notion that nothing can be done – disputing that capitalism as we know it is the best and, in any case, the only possible option. They offer a basis upon which we might greatly expand the boundaries of political debate in the United States and beyond. We hope this work will help catalyze a substantive dialogue about the need for a radically different system and how we might go about building it.

NOTES

1. Tibor Scitovsky, *The Joyless Economy* (New York: Oxford University Press, 1992 revision), 210.

2. Richard Flanagan, *The Narrow Road to the Deep North* (New York: Vintage, 2015).

3. As I reported in 2012 in *America the Possible*, among the 20 most well-to-do democracies, the United States ranks last or close to it in 25 major indicators of national well-being. The measures span economic, social, and political performance, just not environmental. See: James Gustave Speth, *America the Possible: Manifesto for a New Economy* (New Haven: Yale University Press, 2012), 1–2.

4. Speth, *America the Possible*, chapter 4.

5. See Environmental Protection Agency, "National Summary of State Information," https://ofmpub.epa.gov/waters10/attains_nation_cy.control#total_assessed_waters.

6. See American Lung Association, *The State of the Air 2016*, Key Findings, http://www.lung.org/our-initiatives/healthy-air/sota/keyfindings/.

7. See United States Department of Agriculture, Natural Resources Conservation Service, "2012 Natural Resources Inventory," Summary Report, August 2015, http:// www.nrcs.usda.gov/Internet/FSE_DOCUMENTS/nrcseprd396218.pdf.

8. See Matt Lee-Ashley and Nicole Gentile, Center for American Progress, "Confronting America's Wildlife Extinction Crisis," October 2015, https://cdn.americanprogress.org/wp-content/uploads/2015/10/09142515/WildlifeExtinction-report.pdf.

9. Frederick Buell, *From Apocalypse to Way of Life: Environmental Crisis in the American Century* (New York: Routledge, 2004), 3–4, 10.

10. Naomi Oreskes and Erik M. Conway, *Merchants of Doubt: How a Handful of Scientists Obscured the Truth on Issues from Tobacco Smoke to Global Warming* (New York: Bloomsbury, 2010).

11. Judith Layzer, *Open for Business* (Cambridge: MIT Press, 2012), 4.

12. See James Gustave Speth, *Angels by the River: A Memoir* (White River Junction, VT: Chelsea Green Publishing, 2014), 136–37 and the works cited there. And see James Gustave Speth, *The Bridge at the Edge of the World* (New Haven: Yale University Press, 2008), 116–17.

13. See e.g. Speth, *America the Possible*. And see the works cited in notes 14 and 27, below.

14. See generally *Yes!* magazine and www.community-wealth.org. And see Gar Alperovitz, *What Then Must We Do? Straight Talk about the Next American Revolution* (White River Junction, VT: Chelsea Green Publishing, 2013) and *America Beyond Capitalism* (Hoboken, NJ: John Wiley, 2005).

15. Quoted in Lawrence E. Harrison, *The Central Liberal Truth* (Oxford: Oxford University Press, 2006), xvi.

16. Howard Gardner, *Changing Minds: The Art and Science of Changing Our Own and Other People's Minds* (Boston: Harvard Business School Press, 2006), 69, 82. See also James MacGregor Burns, *Transforming Leadership: A New Pursuit of Happiness* (New York: Grove Press, 2003).

17. Bill Moyers, "The Narrative Imperative," TomPaine.com, January 4, 2007, 2, 5, http://www.tom-paine.com/print/the_narrative_imperative.php.

18. Speth, *The Bridge at the Edge of the World*, 163.

19. Mary Evelyn Tucker, *Worldly Wonder: Religions Enter Their Ecological Phase* (Chicago: Open Court, 2003), 9, 43.

20. See Bruce Rich, *To Uphold the World* (Boston: Beacon, 2010); Albert Schweitzer, *Out of My Life and Thought* (New York: Henry Holt, 1933); Aldo Leopold, *A Sand County Almanac* (New York: Oxford, 1949); Thomas Berry (Mary Evelyn Tucker, ed.), *Evening Thoughts* (San Francisco: Sierra Club Books, 2006); E. O. Wilson, *The Creation* (New York: Norton, 2006); and Terry Tempest Williams, *Refuge* (New York: Vintage, 2001). See also Stephen R. Kellert and James Gustave Speth, eds., *The Coming Transformation* (New Haven: Yale School of Forestry and Environmental Studies, 2009).

21. Ed Diener and Martin E. P. Seligman, "Beyond Money: Toward an Economy of Well-Being," *Psychological Science in the Public Interest* Vol. 5, no. 1 (2004), 3–5; Avner Offer, *The Challenge of Affluence* (Oxford: Oxford University Press, 2006), 15–38. See also the diagrams reproduced in Speth, *The Bridge at the Edge of the World*, Chapter 6.

22. United States: Jonathon Porritt, *Capitalism as if the World Matters* (London: Earthscan, 2005), 54; United Kingdom: Nick Donovan and David Halpern, *Life Satisfaction: The State of Knowledge and Implications for Government*, UK Cabinet Office Strategy Unit, December 2002, 17; Japan: Bruno S. Frey and Alois Stutzer, *Happiness and Economics: How the Economy and Institutions Affect Human Well-Being* (Princeton, NJ: Princeton University Press, 2002), 9.

23. Richard A. Easterlin and Laura Angelescu, "Happiness and Growth the World Over: Time Series Evidence on the Happiness-

Income Paradox," Institute for the Study of Labor, Bonn,
Germany, Discussion Paper No. 4060, March 2009.

24. Diener and Seligman, "Beyond Money," 3.

25. Ibid., 10.

26. Quoted in Martin E. P. Seligman, *Flourish* (New York: Free Press,
2011), 20.

27. See, e.g., Juliet Schor, *Plenitude: The New Economics of True Wealth*
(New York: Penguin, 2010); David C. Korten, *The Great Turning*
(San Francisco: Berrett-Koehler, 2006); Duane Elgin, *Voluntary
Simplicity* (New York: Harper, 2010); David Wann, *The New
Normal* (New York: St. Martin's, 2010); Thomas Princen, *Treading
Softly* (Cambridge, MA: MIT Press, 2010); Bill McKibben, *Deep
Economy* (New York: Times Books, 2007); Jay Walljasper, *All That
We Share* (New York: The New Press, 2010); Janelle Orsi and
Emily Doskow, *The Sharing Solution* (Berkeley, CA: NOLO, 2009);
and Fritjof Capra and Hazel Henderson, *Qualitative Growth*
(Institute of Chartered Accountants in England and Wales, jointly
published with Tomorrow's Company, 2009), http://
www.icaew.com/search?q=capra+and+henderson. And see: The
Democracy Collaborative, www. community-wealth.org; Institute
for Local Self-Reliance, https://ilsr.org; Next System Project,
thenextsystem.org; Beautiful Solutions, https://
solutions.thischangeseverything.org; Transition US,
www.transitionus.org; US Solidarity Economy Network, https://
ussolidarityeconomy.word-press.com; BALLE, https://
bealocalist.org.

28. See: www.biophilicdesign.net; Stephen R. Kellert et al., *Biophilic
Design* (New York: Wiley, 2008); Stephen Kellert, *Building for Life*
(Washington, DC: Island Press, 2005); David W. Orr, *The Nature*

of Design (Oxford: Oxford University Press, 2004); and William McDonough and Michael Braungart, *Cradle to Cradle* (San Francisco: North Point Press, 2002).

29. Paul D. Raskin, "The Great Transition Today: A Report from the Future," GTI Paper Series. Frontiers of a Great Transition no. 2 (Tellus Institute, 2006), http://www.greattransition.org/archives/papers/The_Great_Transition_Today.pdf.

30. The presentation is adapted from James Gustave Speth, "Getting to the Next System: Guideposts on the Way to a New Political Economy," The Next System Project Report 2, The Democracy Collaborative, October, 2015, 16–18, https://thenextsystem.org/gettowhatsnext.

31. John Maynard Keynes, "Economic Possibilities for Our Grandchildren," in Keynes, *Essays in Persuasion* (New York: W. W. Norton and Company, 1963 [1933]), 365–373.

PETER DENTON

+ + +

Creation
Ecology

+ + +

Gus Speth's essay "The Joyful Economy: A Next System Possibility" begins by pointing out how the environmental movement in North America over the past 50 years has failed to change the culture it knew was destroying Earth.

As one of the founders of the Natural Resources Defense Council and the World Resources Institute, he has been a leader in this movement. Speth ruefully observes that despite victories in the areas of environmental law, habitat protection and conservation, the destructive trajectory of a culture skewed by profit and driven by perpetual growth has only accelerated toward catastrophe on a planetary scale.

Environmentalist David Suzuki similarly has described the last 50 years of environmentalism in Canada as "a failure" because ecologically destructive systems continue to thrive, largely unhindered, despite his warnings.

Periodic laments for damage will not prevent further losses, however. For Speth, as for Suzuki and other activists, it is long past time for a transformational system change.

Admittedly, "The Joyful Economy" is an idealistic proposal. Anticipating this criticism, Speth argues that without such idealism, the practical problems we face will paralyze us into further inaction. He therefore offers a description of our destination, a vision of what a new system and a new society would be like, rather than a road map detailing how to get there from here.

This is both the strength and weakness of his proposal. Had he offered a map, a chorus of objections would be offered at every point. Yet the destination he identifies, however idealistic, is more desirable than the one that otherwise lies ahead. As he observes, we don't need to do anything to ensure a catastrophic future; the systems we have developed and promoted will surely bring about that nightmare. Only a major system change, grounded in hope, has the potential to avert the inevitable disaster.

Why a joyful economy should matter to Christians

From a Christian perspective, Speth's proposal is ruefully ironic. He offers his personal vision of a new Jerusalem because the Christian communities of North America, like the environmentalists, have failed in their efforts to create one of their own to replace what is crumbling around us.

To sharpen the point, I would argue that the single greatest moral failure of the Christian church in any age is its current response to the climate crisis and its implications. While acknowledging other moral failures of the church across the ages, nothing else matches the scale and consequences of its failure in our generation to live against the culture of planetary devastation that threatens the future of all of the children of Earth. Creation itself is at risk, because of what we are doing and how we are living today, particularly in North America.

Looking for the reasons for our current predicament, it is easily argued that Christianity has not only been complicit in this assault on Creation over the last 400 years, but has actually provided the moral sanction that continues to excuse its defilement and thwart its restoration.

These are not words any Christian wants to hear. They echo the warning, however, that historian of technology Lynn White, Jr., offered in an article published in *Science* in 1967.[1] Taken from an address given to the American Academy of Sciences on Boxing Day in 1966 (and thus probably only to a handful of people), White's thesis has been picked up and elaborated over the past 50 years as a secular critique of Western Christianity.[2]

While the evidence he offered was meagre and the remedy he proposed easily dismissed (remaking Christian theology and society according to the equality of all creatures, modelled on the ideas of St. Francis of Assisi), White's thesis obviously struck a nerve: the impending ecological crisis was the result of a Christian perspective after 1600 that objectified and commodified the natural world, subjecting Nature to the needs and desires of people like us, and blessing those who dominated and destroyed it.

White was a medievalist, so he believed the change took place after Renaissance humanists accepted the Copernican worldview, in which the sun (not the Earth) became the centre of the universe. Displacing the Earth from the centre of everything led to a focus instead on the central importance of "Man," a perspective woven through Protestant theology after the Reformation just as much as it was depicted in Renaissance art and literature.

Nature (and therefore God's Creation) became mere stuff, valuable only in terms of how it could be used by humans. For example, like many others in the Puritan tradition, John Milton interpreted the Book of Genesis this way in *Paradise Lost* (1667), asserting human dominion over all Creation and reducing the natural world to the inanimate stage on which the drama of human history was performed.[3]

With the right tools, Nature could be counted, measured, divided, sold, traded and otherwise treated as a commodity. Its creatures were no different; their purpose was subject to the whims of fashion as much as the needs and desires of a growing global population, fed and fuelled by the spread of European colonial and imperial culture and the economies that drove them.[4] "Subdue the earth" was just as much an ideology of expansion as "go forth and multiply," blessed if not explicitly encouraged by the Christian church. Its members accompanied the expeditions, settlements, and conquests of Empire around the world, offering absolution for sins committed along the way, and capitalizing on its systems to expand the global reach of institutional Christianity, both Protestant and Catholic.

The global industrial economy that now threatens the future of Creation was thus interwoven with the theology and the practice of the Western Christian church from the 17th century onward. For a major system transformation like Speth's "joyful economy" to take place, Western Christians therefore need to engage in a similar theological transformation, as well.

The eco-theologian's tale

White's critique of the environmental flaws in Renaissance Christian theology was offered in the context of a much larger intellectual reconsideration of Christianity in the 1960s and 1970s, undertaken by a host of scholars who explored its culpability for other social and cultural ills of the modern age.

While the publication of Rachel Carson's *Silent Spring* (1962) certainly stirred up interest and concern, the environment was propelled into the headlines only by catastrophes like the Love Canal toxic waste disaster in 1978. There were other, seemingly more urgent social issues with which the Christian church had to wrestle in the meantime, as the world reeled from the Cuban Missile Crisis, muddled through the

Cold War, entered the space race, debated the sexual revolution, and struggled with the Vietnam War, to name just a few of the more prominent distractions.

Social reform was in the air, however. Concerns with its participation in an unjust economic order led to formulations of liberation theology, born in the new base communities of the Roman Catholic church in Central and South America, following Gustavo Gutierrez's book in 1971.[5] Protestants were equally complicit, but it was easier to target an antagonist that had a street address (the Vatican) and a face to go with it (the pope). The idea that Jesus had "a preferential option for the poor" became increasingly part of ecumenical theological conversation, even if the institutional church was uncertain what to do about it.

At the same time, themes from liberation theology were echoed in the rise of the black theology movement, in response to desegregation in the United States and protests against apartheid in South Africa. Black theology ranged widely, from Martin Luther King, Jr., Malcolm X, and Angela Davis; to Desmond Tutu, Allan Boesak and (eventually, upon his release) Nelson Mandela. It wove social, political, racial, and cultural injustice together with religious themes derived from Christian (primarily Protestant) and Islamic tradition, creating a powerful critique of the-world-as-it-is, all framed by the hopeful struggle for liberation and equality.

In both liberation theology and black theology, a better world was not only possible, it was something toward which people could work with the expectation of seeing results in the near future. Progress was discernible and measurable; in the worlds of society and culture, people could make a difference by what they chose to do.

Looking back over the past 50 years, however, those social reformers would likely feel the same today as Gus Speth. There has been significant progress, but not enough. We still seem to live in a world shaped by inequity, undermined by corruption, and run for the benefit of a few – a world where there is debate whether #BlackLivesMatter, and in which the numbers of refugees continues to soar.

Concern about the environmental degradation caused by overconsumption was a natural corollary of these other theological critiques of society and culture. In the 1970s and 1980s, a parallel ecumenical movement within the Western Christian church developed with two main themes related to our place in Nature: creation theology (or spirituality) and the dialogue between science and religion.

Creation theology (or eco-theology) wrestled with the problem of divine immanence, realizing that in the historical concern to ensure Christians were not worshipping trees, the church had lost sight of what it meant to find God in Creation, or in Nature. Similarly, as science (especially physics) looked toward the meaning of things and the origins of the universe, it had long since trespassed into religious territory by the language and concepts it employed. Questions about the relationship between science and religion challenged theologians and scientists alike to engage in common conversation. Add to this mix a growing cross-cultural interest in comparative religion and ecology, manifested in a series of academic and ecumenical conferences,[6] and it meant there was fruitful conversation on what religion and science contributed to our understanding of the meaning of life. The John Templeton Foundation seized on this interest and started a number of significant initiatives in science and religion in the 1990s, funding topics that had only rarely before received financial support from universities or foundations.[7]

Prominent theologians tackled this larger project of merging Christian theology with contemporary science, philosophy, and 20th-century thought in general. Canadian-born Jesuit Bernard Lonergan's *Method in Theology* (1971) was a monumental effort, while German Protestant Jürgen Moltmann wrote a theological series (that included the important *God in Creation*) on current theological subjects, about which Wolfhart Pannenberg also had much to say.[8] In the United States, feminist theologian Sallie McFague shaped the field of metaphorical theology, considering what it meant to be "the body of Christ" in Creation.[9] For those inclined more

JAMES GUSTAVE SPETH & PETER DENTON

to creation spirituality, a rediscovery of Celtic elements provided other expressions of relations with nature, and process theology offered by scholars like John Cobb revived A. N. Whitehead's ideas from earlier in the century.[10]

As a graduate (and theology) student in the 1980s and 1990s, it was a heady time for me. Professors despaired at constructing courses based on reading contemporary theological "classics," because within a year there were three more such books (at least) in any field they wanted to teach. Yet, as the years rolled on, the early momentum in these important fields waned. Looking back, I would have to echo the same lament as Speth and Suzuki, for despite everything that has been written, nothing much has changed. The eco-theologians, like the environmentalists, have failed. The conversation remains deadlocked between dominion and stewardship; between whether Creation is ours to use as we please or whether we have responsibility to manage the natural affairs of the world God has entrusted to our care.[11] A similar impasse has been reached between science and religion, or science and theology.[12] Nor has anything much new been said about ecology and religion recently, from the perspective of any major religious tradition.[13]

All around us, the world moves closer to the brink of disaster, as planetary boundaries are reached and exceeded. Like other players in this global end game, the leaders of the Christian church have become masters of distraction, focusing attention and energy on everything else but the ongoing devastation of God's Creation.

There have been some bright spots, however, perhaps the most important of which was the papal encyclical *Laudato Si'*, issued in 2015 by Pope Francis. While there is nothing radical in the work as a whole, the fact of its existence and papal "authorship" has galvanized more than the Roman Catholic Church to consider not only how we live in Creation, but how we live with each other. Poverty, wealth, and injustice are woven together with both themes from liberation theology and also respect for Pachamama (Mother Earth) no doubt in part thanks to the South American heritage of the current pope.

A modest proposal

While there is insufficient space to develop more than the suggestion here, it seems to me that the moral failure of the Christian church has been reflected more in its practice than in its theology. For the kind of system transformation Speth suggests to succeed, Christians as individuals and as communities of faith need to engage practical ecological concerns at the local level, rethinking lifestyle choices in personal and local community contexts. More theological talk, by itself, is pointless.

Speth's "joyful economy" provides a series of avenues to pursue that local engagement, but the motivation for Christians goes beyond our anxieties about any future world. As a motivator, fear is much less effective than hope. As Speth observes, anxiety and worry are more likely to depress people into inaction. But hope works only as long as there is potential to change; otherwise, it simply turns into deeper despair. Losing hope is worse than having no hope to begin with.

As Christians, our hope needs to be grounded in faith. As the writer of Hebrews reminds us, faith is the "substance of things hoped for, the evidence of things unseen." It is not a product of the marketplace, of political pronouncements, or of scientific assessment.

In our generation, we are being called to have faith that a better future is possible only if we work toward it ourselves. There is no technological shortcut to a new Jerusalem, nor will God solve the problems of Creation for us.

In the face of the environmental catastrophe already beginning to unfold, we must realize the fundamental truth that, by definition, all ecology is local. We have to start living "close to home" if we want a sustainable future; regrettably, our inability to appreciate such wisdom underpins the unsustainable society we have constructed.[14] Ecology never happens somewhere else; what happens around us, right where we are, determines both our health and our future.

To rearrange the words often used into a concept that expresses this wisdom, we need to articulate and practice

"Creation ecology" in the choices we make, throughout the different dimensions of our life as individuals and as communities. Among the myriad terms that have been used to depict theology and ecology, this one seems to be missing. If all ecology is local, then all Creation must be local, too. We don't experience Creation at a distance; it is around us and within us, woven into who and what we were, are, and will become. Creation is experienced here and now, where we stand, where we sit, where we breathe, where we eat. Our home is our experience of Creation; our parish, as Christians, is wherever we live. Creation ecology is an expression of the dynamic presence of God's Spirit within us, all within a universe designed and created as a nexus of relationships by God, one that we simply and wisely call "home."

After all, faith is entirely personal and individual, but it can also be collective and communal. Faith can mobilize whole communities into action, to ends which are both practical and which bring glory to God – and which transform our world in the direction of a sustainable future, one better choice at a time.

Gus Speth's "joyful economy" nicely summarizes what to do and how to do it, close to home. "The Next System Project" is something we should all embrace.

The reasons for joining in such a transformation obviously will be our own, as Christians, but if all those who claimed the Christian faith actually acted on principles of Creation ecology where they lived, Speth's ideal would become real, as the global transformation he describes began to take place.

If we consciously and intentionally lived out those ecological principles toward the destination Speth describes, we would find allies and friends from other religious traditions along the way, who themselves must articulate their own reasons for transformations toward a sustainable future.

In our own way and in our own local places, we would then all be writing together the new Earth story that Passionist priest Thomas Berry considered to be "the great work" of our generation, as within that story of the home in Creation that God intends, we would find room for all the children of Earth.[15]

NOTES

1. Lynn White, Jr, "The Historical Roots of Our Ecologic Crisis," *Science* 155, no 3767 (10 March 1967), 1203–07.

2. Bron Taylor, "The Greening of Religion Hypothesis (Part One): From Lynn White, Jr and Claims That Religions Can Promote Environmentally Destructive Attitudes and Behaviors to Assertions They Are Becoming Environmentally Friendly," *Journal for the Study of Religion, Nature and Culture*, 10.3 (2016), 26–305.

3. Carolyn Merchant, *The Death of Nature: Women, Ecology and the Scientific Revolution* (New York: HarperCollins, 1980); Bill McKibben's *The End of Nature* (New York: Random House, 2006).

4. For an elaboration of this argument, see my *Gift Ecology: Reimagining a Sustainable World* (Victoria, BC: Rocky Mountain Books, 2012), especially Chapter 1 ("The Mechanical 'I'"); Chapter 2 ("The Methodical Muse"); and Chapter 3 ("The Metrical Me").

5. Gustavo Gutierrez, *Teologia de la liberacion: Perspectivas* (Lima: CEP, 1971).

6. Religion of the World and Ecology Conference series, sponsored through the Harvard Divinity School, which later became the Yale Forum on Ecology and Religion, which have been shepherded by Mary Evelyn Tucker and John Grim.

7. The Science and Religion Course Prizes successfully encouraged institutions and faculty alike to develop courses in the subject area (I was fortunate to receive one), but after that initiative ended, the focus of their funding became much more esoteric.

8. Jürgen Moltmann, *God in Creation: An Ecological Doctrine of Creation* (London: SCM Press, 1985); Wolfhart Pannenberg, *Toward a Theology of Nature: Essays on Science and Faith* (Louisville: Westminster/John Knox Press, 1993).

9. Sallie McFague, *Metaphorical Theology: Models of God in Religious Language* (Philadelphia: Fortress Press, 1982); *Models of God: Theology for an Ecological, Nuclear Age* (Minneapolis: Fortress Press, 1987); *The Body of God: An Ecological Theology* (Minneapolis: Fortress Press, 1993); *Life Abundant; Rethinking Theology and Economy for a Planet in Peril* (Minneapolis: Fortress Press, 2001); *A New Climate for Theology: God, the World and Global Warming* (Minneapolis: Fortress, 2003).

10. Woven together by Herbert O'Driscoll in his stories-as-sermons, just as preacher Frederick Buechner made contemporary issues part of a Christian perspective on life together.

11. See, for example, Douglas John Hall, *Imaging God: Dominion as Stewardship* (Grand Rapids; Eerdmans, 1986).

12. Consider, for example, the rich history of the Gifford Lectures in Scotland, and how over the last 20 years they have devolved into more general and popular topics instead of relating religious and scientific ways of knowing.

13. One recent and courageous example of crossing boundaries of religion, culture, and politics on the important subject of ecology and religion was the 2nd International Seminar on Environment, Religion and Culture: Promoting Intercultural Dialogue for Sustainable Development (Tehran, April 2016), sponsored by UNEP, UNESCO, and the government of Iran. I was fortunate to participate, along with Bron Taylor, Mary Evelyn Tucker, John Grim, and a handful of others.

14. For more about this, see my *Technology and Sustainability* (Victoria: Rocky Mountain Books, 2014) and *Live Close to Home* (Victoria: Rocky Mountain Books, 2016).

15. I first learned of Thomas Berry at St. Michael's College (Toronto) by reading his "Riverdale Papers." These were circulated in TypeScript as he was forbidden to publish his ideas about ecology until a theological thaw took place in the late 1980s/ early 1990s. For a good introduction to his thought, see his *The Great Work: Our Way into the Future* (1990; reprinted Toronto: Random House Canada, 2011), and various collections of his essays, edited by Mary Evelyn Tucker and John Grim. Tucker and Grim (along with Andrew Angyal) are also authors of the excellent *Thomas Berry: A Biography* (New York: Columbia University Press, 2019).

JAMES GUSTAVE SPETH

James Gustave "Gus" Speth is a senior fellow at the Vermont Law School and at the Democracy Collaborative, where he serves as co-chair of the Next System Project. In 2009 he completed his decade-long tenure as dean at the Yale School of Forestry and Environmental Studies. From 1993 to 1999, Gus was administrator of the United Nations Development Programme and chair of the UN Development Group. Prior to his service at the UN, he was founder and president of the World Resources Institute; professor of law at Georgetown University; chairman of the U.S. Council on Environmental Quality (Carter Administration); and senior attorney and cofounder, Natural Resources Defense Council.

PETER DENTON

Peter Denton is an ordained minister in the United Church of Canada, with a Ph.D. in religion and social sciences (McMaster). His 30-plus years of interdisciplinary teaching and research have focused on the nexus of science, technology, and society. Adjunct associate professor of history at the Royal Military College of Canada, he is the author or editor of six books, including *Gift Ecology: Reimagining a Sustainable World* (2012), *Technology and Sustainability* (2014) and *Live Close to Home* (2016) and, since 2015, also a regular contributor of pungent op eds to the *Winnipeg Free Press*. Involved in various roles since 2012 with the Civil Society Unit of UN Environment (United Nations Environment Programme), in 2014 he was honoured as an elder among the Maasai for his ongoing development work in Kenya.

The Architecture of Hope
DOUGLAS MACLEOD

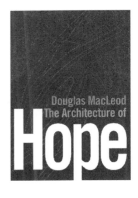

Architect and educator Douglas MacLeod offers a stark and immediately compelling glimpse into the future, 15 years hence, in which we can live and work together to build better communities for tomorrow.

This insightful and compelling book imagines the idea of cooperative communities where people can produce more energy than they use; purify more water than they pollute; grow more food than they consume; and recycle more waste than they produce, with technologies that already exist or that will be within our grasp in a few years.

Most important of all, the people of the community own and profit from these resources.

The Architecture of Hope depicts a way of living that is decentralized, re-localized, and regenerative. And possible.

ISBN 978-1-77343-174-1

80 PAGES, 4.75" X 7" PAPERBACK, $14.95

Pursuit of Virtue
THE PATH TO A GOOD FUTURE
THOMAS LOMBARDO

In *The Pursuit of Virtue*, Lombardo outlines the impact that today's culture of thought is having on us individually and collectively – leaving us compulsively focused on the present, seeking external validation. Lombardo encourages us to choose a path to what he calls a Good Future, by acknowledging and developing our internal resources for wisdom. This Good Future transcends the external and infuses our lives with qualities such as self-evolution, courage, and critical thinking, to lead us out of the shadows and into the light.

ISBN 978-1-77343-152-9

128 PAGES, 4.25" X 6.25" PAPERBACK, $12.95

For Everything a Season

THE WISDOM OF TRADITIONAL VALUES IN TURBULENT TIMES

WARREN JOHNSON

For Everything a Season reignites the sacred flame. Warren Johnson urges us to recommit to faith, while maintaining our reason. Guided by traditional principles embedded in the great teachings of the New and Old Testaments, he offers a hopeful path to creating a modern eco-system where every individual consumes and creates in balance with the sacred whole. In this way, we do away with excess, make reparations for our past, and ultimately lead a happier, healthier life.

ISBN 978-1-77343-166-6

96 PAGES, 4.25" X 6.25" PAPERBACK, $12.95

The Voice of the Galilean

THE STORY OF A LIFE, A JOURNEY, A DISCOVERY, A GIFT, AND A FATE

REX WEYLER

Rex Weyler's *The Voice of the Galilean* stands as one of the most clear, compelling, and concise tellings of the life and teachings of Jesus ever written. Excerpted and updated from his seminal book *The Jesus Sayings: The Quest for His Authentic Message* – a brilliant synthesis of the work of international Bible scholars and some 200 ancient sources, including the gospels of Thomas and Mary –*The Voice of the Galilean* distills the teachings of Jesus with crystal clarity, sensitivity, insight, and passion. Equally important, Weyler challenges readers to bear "witness" to Jesus' message today, in their own lives.

ISBN 978-1-77343-155-0

96 PAGES, 4.25" X 6.25" PAPERBACK, $12.95

In the Face of Fear
ON LAUGHING ALL THE WAY TO WISDOM
WALTER G. MOSS

Take a moment and picture South African Archbishop Desmond Tutu and Buddhist spiritual leader the Dalai Lama together. There's a good chance the image that comes to mind is one where they're both smiling, if not outright laughing. These two stalwart individuals of faith have faced more fear than many humans will ever know, and yet somehow they have arrived at a place where their automatic response is to emit a sound that lightens both heart and mind – laughter. This, says author Walter G. Moss, is the pure product of applied wisdom. Profound yet lighthearted, with an eclectic devotional edge that will keep you off guard, *In the Face of Fear* emboldens us to shrug off our self-imposed seriousness in favour of a light touch. Doing so, could do more to cast light on what's possible than stumbling around in the dark.

ISBN 978-1-77343-160-4

96 PAGES, 4.25" X 6.25" PAPERBACK, $12.95

Creative Aging

STORIES FROM THE PAGES OF
THE JOURNAL "SAGE-ING"

CAROLYN COWAN & KAREN CLOSE

Creative Aging is a powerful social and cultural movement that is stirring the imaginations of communities and people everywhere. Often called Sage-ing, it takes many forms: academic, social, and personal. Sage-ing is about seeking – satisfying inner gnawing and transforming it to knowing and action. Aging can be alchemy when one allows the realization that to know thyself and contribute that knowing to our culture is indeed one of life's highest purposes. That knowing brings the gratitude, grace, and integrity that a life deserves. The creative journey into self is a strong aid to health and well-being for the individual and to culture.

ISBN 978-1-77064-790-9

320 PAGES, 6" X 9" PAPERBACK, $24.95

Activist Alphabet
DONNA SINCLAIR

Donna Sinclair's book *Activist Alphabet* is an effort to figure out why and how activists fall passionately in love with a cause, a watershed, or a planet and its people. It's a primer, or an alphabet, on how to stay strong enough to keep putting that love into action, over and over. As author Donna Sinclair explains, it is particularly aimed at people of faith, because love, we say, is what we are about, even though it makes us terribly vulnerable to grief and loss. Good and evil, we say, is what we are about, even though that calls us to study and learn and intervene, trying to protect. Trying to find hope. Trying to see where God fits and lifts in the current chaos.

ISBN 978-1-77343-154-3

176 PAGES, 5.5" X 8.5" PAPERBACK, $19.95

WOOD LAKE

IMAGINING, LIVING, AND TELLING
THE FAITH STORY.

WOOD LAKE IS THE FAITH STORY COMPANY.

It has told
- the story of the seasons of the earth, the people of God, and the place and purpose of faith in the world;
- the story of the faith journey, from birth to death;
- the story of Jesus and the churches that carry his message.

Wood Lake has been telling stories for more than 35 years. During that time, it has given form and substance to the words, songs, pictures, and ideas of hundreds of storytellers.

Those stories have taken a multitude of forms – parables, poems, drawings, prayers, epiphanies, songs, books, paintings, hymns, curricula – all driven by a common mission of serving those on the faith journey.

WOOD LAKE PUBLISHING INC.

485 Beaver Lake Road, Kelowna, BC, Canada v4v 1s5

250.766.2778

www.woodlake.com